01 May

FHM

HAMPSHIRE COUNTY COUNCIL

WITHDRAWN

KT-513-923

deleted.

Get **more** out of libraries

**Please return or renew this item by the last date shown.**

**You can renew online at www.hants.gov.uk/library**

**Or by phoning  0845 603 5631**

Hampshire
County Council

C015498303

# THE NECESSITY OF POVERTY

## JOHN BIRD

QUARTET

First published in 2012 by Quartet Books Limited
A member of the Namara Group
27 Goodge Street, London W1T 2LD
Copyright © John Bird 2012
The right of John Bird to be identified
as the author of this work has been asserted
by him in accordance with the
Copyright, Designs and Patents Act, 1988
All rights reserved.
No part of this book may be reproduced in
any form or by any means without prior
written permission from the publisher
A catalogue record for this book
is available from the British Library
ISBN 978 0 7043 7303 7
Typeset by Josh Bryson
Printed and bound in Great Britain by
T J International Ltd, Padstow, Cornwall

To the memory of Terry Monaghan (1944–2011) who got me thinking, and to the children of the poor who are made poorer by bad business, poor government and inept giving. Hopefully better business, wiser government and smarter giving will reverse the damage done by others.

# CONTENTS

# 1
# LAZY UNDERWEAR

One Sunday afternoon while walking along the boardwalk in Venice, California, I noticed ahead of me young girls and boys with their pants hanging down. You could see their underwear.

I was spending the afternoon with one of LA's most prominent homeless voices, an African-American advocate who had spent decades fighting for the right of the poor to live among the rich and to be allowed some prosperity.

I asked this man, 'What was it with the underwear?'

'It's simple. The young go and see their brothers in the prison. There, they're wearing these denims that slip off their butts. Why? Because "one size fits all" are issued by the prison and they don't give you belts. So the young imitate their elders. At least that's how it started.'

I was astonished. Many years before, I had been in a boy's correctional facility and we had the same problem. But no fashion grew out of it.

Clothes, as well as music and attitude, seem so finely honed to imitate the poor of the world, especially inner city black culture, that a number of industries desperately need the poor to come up with the best tunes and the coolest fashion.

Poverty is necessary. If the poor did not live on the edge of things – and out of it produce clothes, style and music

– you would not have modern pop culture. You would perhaps have a bland middle class pop, but not one that sought to simulate the desperate words and music of inner city poverty.

The love affair that young middle class white children have with their poor inner black counterparts has produced an enormous industry. It has enriched numerous people in the process: the record companies, producers, promoters and also many of the artists that have grown out of this. Poverty, a launch pad for many, has become the primary source of their prosperity.

On the day that Martin Luther King's house was firebombed in Montgomery, Alabama, Elvis Presley went into the studio to record *Blue Suede Shoes*. The song put Presley on the road to fame and fortune. Up until that year, though, he was a regional singer with a limited appeal. Then he signed up for RCA, leaving Sam Philips Sun records, and the rest is history. From then on, the poor boy from Memphis, Tennessee, was on the way to becoming one of the biggest grossing artists of all time.

Presley was unique for a young performer from the American South. He did not limit himself to the white repertoire. He sang and imitated young black music and style from the start. He wore his hair and clothing the way young black men did in the streets and neighbourhoods around him. Presley soaked up the black experience and out of that made his name and reputation.

Presley came out of poverty and used the music of poverty. The mix of poor white and poor black helped to propel into existence an enormous industry that rolls on today.

Without poverty, without the ingrained oppression of the black experience in the Americas, one cannot imagine what culture would have replaced it. Imagine the world without the slave trade and the Middle Passage that brought black slavery to America. Imagine the world without the musical and cultural descendents of that experience.

I rest my case: much of the modern world would look totally different if we did not have poverty. We live this cultural need for poverty. Even the baby boomers would have been lost without that music to stimulate them. Imagine the swinging sixties without poverty, or without the music that came out of poverty.

The first time I heard the Rolling Stones, I was in a reformatory. One of the boys had been brought back for misbehaving and he had a record with him. It was a demo of *Come On* by the then unknown Rolling Stones. I listened to it and got to like it. When it was released, it did reasonably well. Those that followed did spectacularly well. Later, I heard the original by Chuck Berry and preferred it. But it was the Stones' version that made the major musical change and helped build our modern pop culture.

Using the music of the poor, black South was the basis on which the largely middle class Rolling Stones could become one of the biggest rock bands of all time. They sung black music and sold it back to the young whites of the States. Without the trials and tribulations of America's poor we would not have had the Beatles, the Stones and countless other acts. There would be less fun without poverty to provide the grit and the story line, the passion and the outrage, that informed and empowered musicians without that experience.

*The Necessity of Poverty* is what I call this manifesto. I believe only by understanding how poverty is the backbone of our market-driven lives will we ever get to the bottom of dismantling it. We must understand how poverty provides for us and how without understanding its hold over us, we will never control and defeat poverty, let alone make a few dents in it.

Over the next pages, I hope to demonstrate that we can do something practical and useful about poverty. We can begin to dismantle its effects, but it will take an intellectual revolution in our thinking.

# 2
# THE MARKET IS US

Much of the talk about poverty today is about the enormous gap between rich and poor. People are obsessed with this gap being an indicator of how screwed up the world is. But who creates this gap? Where does the gap appear from?

My father, though a hard-working building labourer, increased the gap between rich and poor virtually every day of his working life. He did this by buying the products of very rich men. For instance, the products created by Edward Guinness, first Earl of Iveagh.

When Lord Iveagh of the Guinness family died in 1923, he left the largest sum of any legacy in Britain. Lord Iveagh was what you might call a 'sliver capitalist'. 'Sliver capitalism' allows a modicum of money to be collected from every transaction. Much modern capitalism is about collecting together lots of pennies and cents.

Most of Iveagh's money came from getting people like my father to drink his beers, which my father did on as many occasions as his working life and finances afforded him. In many ways, Lord Iveagh received the lion's share of my father's weekly wages, with Dad spunking away on average about forty percent in various pubs around London's then-slummy Notting Hill.

## THE NECESSITY OF POVERTY

Lord Iveagh and the Guinness family got richer and out of the contributions from the likes of my father they went on holidays, bought race horses, attended public schools and in an act of beneficence built houses for the working class. The gap between rich and poor increased inexorably, because people like my father bought the products of the one percenters of their generation.

My father and mother, not content to make money available for the Guinness family's race horses and art collections, alighted on another beneficent giver to patronise. Aside from the Guinnesses, the other 'sliver capitalist' that they had a lot of time for was the Bristol based business W.D & H.O. Wills, who made cigarettes and rolling tobacco. My parents had a constant supply of Wills products in the house and about their persons.

Up in the centre of Bristol at the university, you will see a monument to cigarette smoking and all of the advantages it provides. Here is the Wills Memorial Building, where students can study and advance their abilities, courtesy of my father and mother, among others. If you want to see how good cigarette smoking is for you, visit Bristol and see the fine university, which is among the best in the world.

Alas, my mother and father are with us no more, having died early from cancer and heart problems related to the way they splashed their money around and who they chose to patronise. But at least I can go to Bristol University, or look at the stock shares of Guinness – now part of Diageo – and know that their efforts were not in vain. For my parents helped to build some of the biggest stock market performers. They helped to create profits, playing an essential role in making a new generation of one percenters.

Without poverty, cigarette and alcohol fortunes would not have been built and the foundation stones of much of the modern world of big business would not exist.

Some might say therefore, 'Thank God for poverty'. Thank God the poor need to obliterate much of their down time with drink or stimulants and in the process expand the gap between rich and poor.

I was no different from my parents. From the moment I had a penny in my pocket, I was spending it on some family to make them richer. I gave it to merchants who needed lots of little people like me to make them big and grand and capable of living in gated communities or country estates.

I smoked and I drank. Later, moving into the age of computers and the internet, I helped create new one percenters, like Steve Jobs at Apple and Jeff Bezos at Amazon.

My children shopped at Sir Philip Green's emporia – Topshop, Next, etc. – and so played their part in paying for the vastly expensive birthday party Sir Phillip recently flung for his daughter. He flew in pop stars and personalities, much to the chagrin of the Occupy movement and the rest of those outraged at the unfair and uneven levels of wealth distribution.

So, when I hear about the increasing gap between rich and poor, I know that my family and I have done our bit to increase that gap. Until my family and I change our buying patterns the gap will remain and will increase.

## THE NECESSITY OF POVERTY

Buying is no different from that other great democratic mass action we participate in: voting. When we buy a product from a company – Apple, Amazon, Topshop – we are supporting them and increasing their owners' or managers' wealth. We endorse them although we may not like how they spend the money we give them for their products.

When discussing the gap between rich and poor, we must factor ourselves into the equation – our family, friends, acquaintances and every other purchaser in the world. That means factoring in one simple thing: it is not the one percenters who create much of the gap between rich and poor. It is our buying patterns. It is our commitment to products and to brands.

Over last Christmas, Britain's biggest supermarket chain, and the third largest in the world, Tesco, got a drubbing from their customers. Five billion pounds worth of business just did not turn up. This led to an unprecedented fall of eighteen percent in the price of Tesco shares, which terrified the Tesco board and its owners. The involved one percenters were given a financial kicking and have been running around trying to win back their supremacy in the marketplace ever since. But to no avail.

Where is the power in the relationship between the business and the customer? Where does the real power lie? I would suggest that as in earlier times with my parents, so now, we are busily putting coins into the coffers of people who we then blame.

The blaming seems to get us nowhere. So is it not time to use our power? The collective power that turned a former

8

trader like Woolworths into yesterday's news. The power to decide who the new Woolworths might be.

They know their future wealth lies in our hands. And we, the producers of this vast wealth, must decide how to wield that power.

If we are concerned about this gap between rich and poor, we should do something about it. The first thing is not to waste our energies on merely being angry at the situation. Our anger suits the vastly wealthy because it allows us to let off steam. However, using our purchasing power against them hits them hard.

In medieval times, kings made fortunes and distributed wealth, mainly to their barons and knights. Wealth was tied up in land and the incomes garnered from the land. But with the advent of the growing markets, where trade was with strangers and not between known parties, the market became impersonal.

You make things. You bring them to the market. And you convince enough people to buy them. You walk away, often with a sliver of profit, but enough slivers accrue into a fine fortune.

All of this would not be possible if it were not for the essence of the marketplace and why the marketplace actually works: that is the 'you and I's' of former times.

Woolworths didn't fail because its owners stopped liking the colour of our money. Woolies failed because it did not supply the right stuff for our tastes.

It's happening to Marks & Spencer. It will happen to Apple one day. It will happen to almost everyone who raises his profile in the marketplace. There comes a time when our tastes and desires move on. And then fortunes are broken. And they, like the owners of Woolworths, will become the wealthy of yesterday.

You want to do something about this gap, which many of you see as a moral crisis? Then organise. Build the big collectivist consumer groups that will kick a hole through our current buying practises. Let's make shopping a political and social justice issue. Let us take fair trade mainstream. It can no longer hide on the edges.

About five years ago, my daughter and I started a loyalty card that supported thousands of small high street businesses. Its slogan, 'Every little shop helps', was designed to protect our local high street against the big supermarkets who destroy rather than nurture communities.

On average, eighteen percent of ever pound you spend at a supermarket chain remains in the community. If you shop locally, eighty percent of every pound stays in the community. Therefore if you shop locally, you are nurturing communities and creating a diverse marketplace. You are spreading the money about. If you are concerned with not enriching people who throw wild outrageously expensive parties then you need to change the way you buy. And you need to find a way of changing the power bases in purchase.

Or rather use our powerbase as the true 'wealth makers' to break up the monopoly patterns of shopping that create the big gap.

The experiences of our local loyalty card taught us that unless you change those buying patterns, rather than simply disrupt them by the usual politics of protest and occupation, then little will change.

Until fair trade flows into the mainstream, it will remain an important and interesting experiment. Despite achieving its goals on a small scale, only by being embraced by the majority will it have the effects we desire.

With some notable exceptions all wealth at some stage passes through the marketplaces that supply us with goods and services. Until those marketplaces are changed to reflect our rejection of that division of society into the extremely rich and the majority poor, nothing will change. Indeed, the division will expand. Until we build big new social and trade alliances and transform them into political bodies, we will be angry and right but without impact.

The Occupy movement proves that many of us do not want to accept poverty and financial disproportion without struggle. The big reality is that we are building a marketplace of wealth imbalances, and it is our fault if we don't change it.

As well as supporting the incredibly wealthy, my father also put food on the table of the poor. He bought stuff. Even though he had little money, he helped other poor people and other poor people helped him. Through the fully functioning capitalist economy my father, while paying Lord Iveagh's family, supported workers throughout the world. For my father bought stuff that paid the wages, however meagre, of the labourers who produced the goods.

So as well as helping to widen the gap between rich and poor my father, mother and I all put food on the table of workers picking bananas in Central America, tea pickers in Kenya and India, rubber harvesters in Malaya.

If we have the enormous power to make the fortunes of the one percenters, think of the power we have to put food into the mouths of the poor. How? By going out to the local shop or supermarket and buying stuff. Our greatest strength does not lie in our power to vote or protest, but in our power as consumers.

We are the main drivers. Our appetites and needs decide who does well in this world. With such power in our hands, we must use it wisely.

The political forces we need to build for today and tomorrow cannot be mired in moralistic anger and protest. We must be astute and fully aware how markets work and how they can be changed.

If you doubt the power of big numbers, look at the last two hundred years of history. Big numbers through the Labour Movement brought Capitalism to the negotiating table. Big numbers brought the end of American segregation and its South African equivalent, apartheid.  Our own welfare state became possible only when a groundswell of people voted in the post-war radical government. The political system tends to turn and embrace change when big numbers come into play. When progressive beliefs are held by a tiny minority, change is rarely achieved. When political dissent and social demands enter the bloodstream of society, change is often inevitable.

Let us not fool ourselves, though, that mass action always brings change. The first political action I got involved in was 'The Campaign for Nuclear Disarmament' in 1961, and we still have not ended the threat of nuclear war. The mass protests and mass opposition failed to galvanise the majority, hence its continued marginality.

Don't put all your eggs in one basket. We need to fight against both the iniquities of Third World debt and the stagnation of average wages for countless workers, white collar as well as blue, in developed countries. These big issues need to be fought and opposed as a part of the repertoire of opposition along with the misuse and abuse of the government and its hangers on, the governmental contractors. Vast fortunes are being amassed through the spending and awarding of government money. The old adage 'if you want to get rich, get a government contract' holds now more than ever, especially as governments have tried to privatise much of its activity.

More than anything we have to be aware of where the power is in the political, economic and social system. And who creates that power: us. Our quiescence ignores our leverage. Leaving it to a minority to take issue on the big issues is the reason for the perpetuation of the human rights outrages that hover in the background of the growing gap between rich and poor.

The recent Tesco figures reveal a pattern that explains the obvious:

> Turnover: £55 billion.
> Profits: £5 billion.

Dividends: £2.5 billion.
Wages bill: £22 billion.
Directors and Top Management bill:
£100 million.

The obvious is that the £55 billion turnover is the big and important number. That is where Tesco's power lies, not in the £2.5 billion to its shareholders or the £100 million to its few hundred directors and top managers. It may be insulting that £20 billion of wages is divided out to thousands of workers, none of them cashing in on the feeding frenzy at the top, but where is the leverage here? Surely the greatest piece of leverage, as happened over last Christmas, is the withdrawal of buying power. Don't buy if you don't like. Go elsewhere.

A problem throws itself up when you withdraw purchase from a business like Tesco. People, largely the general workforce, find themselves out of work or working harder for less money or, as is the new trend, on short time. Economic activity may mean a lessening of the money you might for instance spend on a daughter's twenty-first birthday in the super rich class – e.g. Sir Philip Green – but it immediately translates itself into a hit on the shop floor.

That is why we need to seriously challenge the way that trade unions are allowed to function – or not function, as the case may be. In a new world of utilising the power of the consumer, trade unions could become supreme. They are already one of the big aggregators of individuals that do not necessarily get included in decision making. Governments and businesses only respond to them when they strike or threaten to.

Unions could develop into trading arms, as their forerunners did in the Cooperative Movement of the 19th century. Disparate working men once banded together to buy, to influence prices and to wring concessions out of suppliers who could not treat organized workers in the same way. We can do this again. Don't forget our history.

I raise this issue because of the need to support new ways of distributing the wealth accumulated by mass purchasing. Much of that wealth should go back to the workforce and the best way for this to reach deep into the system is to create a more equitable distribution system. Tesco is nothing more than a distribution system. Why can't some of our big unions become distribution systems?

Tesco makes nothing other than profit from its power as a distribution system. It does not make the yoghurt. It does not make the shopping trolley you put it in. It does not make the till at the checkout. Often its buildings are owned by third parties. Tesco is a very large version of someone who buys an orange, employs underpaid workers to sell it to you and keeps the profit for himself. Not bad, but not especially good for you.

Trade unions are a good place to begin this new intervention in the 'redistribution of distribution'. This is the area where we can address our power. This is where we need to wield our formidable power as aggregators. The right combination of forces wins wars, e.g. The Red Army. The right combination puts the Beatles at the top of the pops. And the right (or possibly wrong) aggregation makes a new J.K Rowling out of the author of *Fifty Shades of Grey*.

Aggregation, aggregation, aggregation: it's the name of the game. The Arab Spring, however it finally comes to rest, was a supreme example of how combinations make history, markets and military juntas move.

Why did the landed and political interests of the early 19th century transport a group of men from Tolpuddle in Dorset to Australia? Because the vested interests could see the power of 'Combination', calling their legal, parliamentary response *The Combination Acts*. Let the rulers combine, but not the working man. Let landowners, merchants and MP's combine, but not the working people and small farmers.

We need a new Combination of trade unionists, small shop keepers, small suppliers, working farmers, consumers, political and social activists to redistribute the distribution. So that you end up with a social Tesco and a more bio-diverse marketplace.

It is you, me and Aunt Gladys who make the difference. Let us now combine to change governments and marketers. Let's make buying and selling a conscious and powerful act. And not rely on our anger and hatred of a system that kills, maims and makes hunger universal.

# 3
# THE WHIP HAND

When the late Steve Jobs launched his first iPad it seemed a wonder. Many of us rushed out and bought one. I use it to write on and to do drawings on and have even had an exhibition based on the work I created.

Whatever was said about the product on the day of launch its features and ingredients were discussed at great length. Except for one feature, which was as essential as good design and performance. This feature, if mentioned, can be disruptive and painful for us Apple-lovers to absorb. This feature is poverty.

Without poverty, and the history of poverty, Steve Jobs would have been hard pressed to sell more than a handful of his new devices. To take it mainstream, or to a large enough consumer base, meaning that for a short while Apple became America's biggest business, they needed a 'good price'. And a 'good price' meant finding poor people to make it.

Apple could have gone anywhere in its home country to make the iPad. But that would have limited its ability to sell to a mass market. So Apple went to China, a country that knows poverty and has a disciplined (i.e. strictly controlled) and highly talented pool of labour. And to a business, Foxconn, that knew how to deliver the product cheaply.

## THE NECESSITY OF POVERTY

Without poverty, gadgets of the modern world would be at an astronomic price. We would not see the mass spread of new technology and we would not have seen such keen pricing. Poverty, or the fear of it, works wonders to keep costs down.

The existence of poverty ensures that we do not pay more than we would reasonably like for many things. Whether it is a battery chicken at Tesco or a laptop from Apple, the same rules apply: keep the supply contract price keen. Keep the price keen. Keep the costs down and profits up.

Labour is made the cheapest part of the supply chain and workers the least valued.

Therefore, not only do we need poverty, we need the one percenters to force down the cost of labour. We need them to discipline the poor on our behalf.

I want to make art. I want to use the latest means of drawing with the iPad. I therefore need Apple to make sure that, through its suppliers, no one is paid much and everyone at the bottom puts in the hours. I may not want to know the details, but I am lost without this 'necessity of poverty'.

When Steve Jobs died there were reports that some of the Occupy protestors had a minute's silence for him. It may or not be true. But I have had talks with supporters of the Occupy movement who were saddened by his death. As many of us were. But wasn't Jobs, in the final analysis, a one percenter?

Surely one could have kept a personal vigil for the death of any man in his prime being struck down by his particular disease, but that is personal. When you are making politics and political statements, and advocating a different way of running the world, I suggest we need to be conscious of our actions. And our love of Steve Jobs contradicts – I suggest – what the Occupy movement sets out to be: a morally outraged force against excessive wealth accumulation.

Steve Jobs produced some good stuff in his life that may in some way make us all richer creatively, but let us not be ignorant of how he used poverty. Let us not keep our eyes closed to this major contradiction: a great man may make great stuff, but he needs poverty to achieve his goal. Let's not be dreamy about this fact.

I have no problem with people commemorating the passing of a great businessman from the scene. But I would suggest that a deeper grasp of economics and marketplaces would probably not go amiss.

When I spoke recently at a business event, a Occupy supporter asked what her movement should do next. I said, 'Get closer to understanding how capitalism and marketplaces work. Understand the importance of poverty in our own lives. Become cognisant of the system that you wish to change. You need to know how something works before you change it.'

Understand that we create the big fortunes of the one percenters, but understand as well the role of poverty in our economic lives.

Poverty is the backbone of the marketplace. It is not an aberration; it is not a side issue. It is not the unfortunate collateral damage and foundation of the marketplace.

19

## THE NECESSITY OF POVERTY

It is one of the essential ingredients in the way economies perform. Without it we have a different marketplace. And we have a smaller marketplace.

As I have tried to show above, poverty creates the opportunity for us all to buy stuff that we could not normally afford. We would not buy a computer and participate in the technology revolution if it were not for the way that the price of the product falls within our budget. If the price of a product is high because of labour costs then it limits the take up, which limits the development of the marketplace. This limits the technological development trail. Poverty holds down the costs sufficiently to boost market share and create bigger markets.

If we are to realign the world politically and socially, we need to understand how poverty plays an enormous part in our everyday life. It is not enough to be angry with the world of big business and the widening gap between rich and poor. We have to study a system that involves us and that we are complicit in.

The 'necessity of poverty' runs like a thread through the whole of our lives. It keeps our budgets down. And it ensures that even in developed countries costs are kept lower through the intervention of the poorer members of society.

We find it in hotels, where underpaid workers keep room prices down and profits up. Low wages ensure that someone will invest in hotel ownership. We find it as well in the wages of a street cleaner, a factory worker, a transport worker, and a postal worker.

# THE WHIP HAND

The right-wing press loves to get upset when, for instance, the leader of the train drivers union, Bob Crowe, has the effrontery to get his members a professional wage. Surely, today's economy dictates, trains should be run by cheaper workers, who live at the bottom of the pecking order. And when drivers suggest they may withdraw their labour it is considered divisive and selfish. Shareholders withdraw their finances, and international speculators move their money away. Thus, a working man is denied what is often his only creditable bargaining chip.

All of this I suggest is a kind of acceptance of the need to keep costs down even in the developed countries, so that the cost will not be passed on to the consumer. We know if you pass the cost onto the consumer, businesses will not make so many sales. A defence of the consumer, a support of the consumers' interest, justifies paying workers (even though they are also consumers) less.

And this cost control is beneficial to us, who trade on this 'necessity of poverty'.

Poverty draws all consumers into the equation of using poverty to the consumers' advantage. It does not matter how rich or poor the consumer is they are being advantaged by someone else's poverty.

Poverty is the missing ingredient in the world of Apple, in the creation of it, and in the creations of the materials that are used to make it. Steel and other materials are all price sensitive. So however much you may improve certain stages of production, as Apple has tried to do with its products, the raw materials still keep that relationship with poverty real.

## THE NECESSITY OF POVERTY

Why? Because some of the worst human rights and poverty issues on the planet are found in the extraction industries. When mine-owners save money by ignoring the safety of their workers, no one notices. When a mine collapses, trapping and killing workers underground, we feign outrage.

Apple has tried to insist that Foxconn pay better wages and reduce some of the constraints placed on Chinese workers. Constraints have caused some workers to commit suicide or attempt it, but they remain in place.

The poor are in the providing chain at all levels. And we, if we are to realign wealth will need to recognise that role of the poor in our prosperity, however limited it is.

As I have said, much has been done by the Fair Trade movement, and we should support its efforts. But until fair trade becomes mainstream, there will be little evidence of us dismantling the need for the poor to support us in our needs. Only by bringing fair trade into the big arenas of business and economic activity will we be able to reduce the gap between rich and poor. Instead of abhorring it, we can narrow it, or even destroy it.

# 4
# POVERTY USERS

One summer's afternoon when I was fourteen a kindly policeman took me from Chelsea police station to Oxford Detention Centre. Earlier, a prominent juvenile magistrate had sentenced me to a 'short, sharp shock'. Today you would not get away with the state sponsored terrorism handed out to young working class boys who had fallen into crime.

The principle behind it was to shock you out of wrongdoing. We might now call it a boot camp, but not of an improving kind. It was a regime of violence and lock ups with a heavy emphasis on sport and exercise and doing exactly as you were told. Beatings were handed out indiscriminately.

By fourteen, I had a string of court appearances for offences that would now warrant a caution. In 1960 our class divided world had yet to evolve liberal attitudes towards the poor and needy. Sociologists and psychologists were rare in prisons, and correctional systems sought to straighten out the overwhelmingly poor of society.

The policeman, who was young, had recently joined the force. He was living in police barracks, but was saving to marry his fiancée. So even though he had done a full duty, that day he volunteered to do some overtime by taking me to Oxford.

He took all the overtime that was available and I was a part of his plan of bringing that wedding day nearer, when he could marry and get a police flat. He talked happily about his plans, and I was intrigued by how devoted he was to getting married and starting a family.

He delivered me to Oxford and there I continued my education. Three months later, I was out ready to do more harm and provide more overtime for another police officer. I remained in that system, providing work for policemen, court officials, magistrates, judges, and drivers of police waggons for a good few years. Civil servants in the Home Office and in the vast mechanism called the Justice Service worked flat out for us.

Without kids like us, many working class policemen and middle class magistrates, judges, clerks, barristers, etc. would be out of work. And many MPs would not get the chance to wax lyrical about crime and what needed to be about it. And many newspapers would not enjoy circulation because they could not report on crime.

A whole world of activity hid behind my simple act of being a part of the problem of post-war Britain. And proving the 'necessity of poverty' for thousands upon thousands of people. We, the criminal underclass, were one of the biggest job and wealth creation schemes imaginable. Without the crime industry, much of business and commerce would be hard pressed to keep so many people in work.

Crime keeps people in work. A well-behaving world would mean countless lay offs. University sociology departments would shrivel up. Architects of prisons and court houses would have to go back to the drawing board. Prosperity would be truncated for a vast army of workers and professionals. And hundreds of billions of pounds of governmental money would go unused because we had somehow sorted out the relationship between poverty and crime.

Wrongdoing in all of its forms is the goose that lays the golden egg. Reputations and TV programmes can get made out of wrongdoing. And busying themselves underneath it all are the private security companies, the prison creators and administrators, the myriad lives of people who desperately hang on to this 'necessity of poverty'.

Of course with the growing dislocation of the middle classes, with their desperate need not to be middle class, there has been a better quality of education finding their way into the prison system. Drugs, the swinging sixties and the advent of drug inspired music, have all added to an increasing lawlessness as people from the middle class have opted for crime. But this is still a small part of the large army of wrongdoers who still largely are recruited from the working, or increasingly, the 'workless' class.

If poverty is the backbone of the economic system then poverty is also a deciding factor in the criminal justice industry.

The crime and wrongdoing industry is an obvious beneficiary of poverty. If that seems unlikely to you, think of society and who else needs poverty to prosper.

We need the poor to keep our costs down. We need the poor to give us work. But are there other ways that we need the poor?

## THE NECESSITY OF POVERTY

The greatest benefits of poverty accrue to the health industry (Britain's biggest employer), the drug companies and the hundreds of providers who supply our hospital system with many of their needs: buildings, heating, plastic cups, surgical gloves, instruments, beds, cleaning products, ambulances, etc.

Much of the prosperity of Britain and the lives of the many are tied up with the army of people involved in illness and providing for the ill. Illness has a direct relation to poverty.

When the National Health Service and Welfare State were envisaged they had a decided class flavour to them. The middle and upper classes could always provide for themselves. They had their nest eggs and insurance. Because they did not do such onerous tasks, they tended not to harm themselves through work.

Added to this they had stability and prosperity and did not weigh themselves down with palliatives and escapes. They did not go for instant gratification and drunkenness in the same proportions as the largely unstable working and social conditions of much of the labouring poor.

Middle class housing was superior to that of most of the poor. And the quality of their food was better than what working people had to eat.

The middle classes have largely been socially conditioned to be modest in all things, and even though the hungry thirties knocked many of them into 'almost poverty' they struggled on with the 'modesty' mantra.

So when the mild middle class socialists of the Labour Government, building on the work of the wartime government and the Beveridge Report, launched the Welfare State it was to enfranchise the poor into a better world. A world of good housing, good education and good health.

Many of the arguments around the creation of the NHS revolved around getting people to be better in themselves: to eat better, exercise better, live better. Not to destroy themselves with bad food, alcohol and cigarettes. Education around health and personal responsibility was one of the biggest elements of those early days, which I well remember. You drank state provided milk. You took vitamins. Everywhere there were posters advising you on how to be healthier. And you exercised continuously. Hopefully you would also eat better food and spend your money more wisely and not do as my post war father did and spunk it away in the pub.

The middle classes in many ways already had their own welfare state in the sense that they could provide for themselves. They put a bit aside for a rainy day. They had their doctors and they had their housing and their nutrition.

So the big plan was to morph the working poor into better health and wellbeing. So the NHS was intended as a health service, not a 'sick service', which is what it has become.

Over the years the struggle for self-health, the way that the middle classes acted, went on the back burner. And an increasing number of people relied on the NHS to 'bring them back to health', rather than prevent them from getting unhealthy.

## THE NECESSITY OF POVERTY

The poor were less likely to become self-healers. So the NHS grew obese to accommodate people needing to be brought back to health because of poor nutrition, poor exercise and an overwhelming dependency on palliatives. The original NHS was put on hold and a new 'consumerist' health service came into being. A health service that was an adjunct of the marketplace where you required a 'service' and you were supplied as a customer. A customer of a service that would not ask of you that you kept yourself healthy. But a business that simply provided you with the means to bring you back to health, health that you may well have damaged yourself.

Related to the changing Health Service was a changing class structure. The working class was increasingly moving into the middle classes. Much menial work was largely done by overseas labour. After Thatcher's dismantling of the Lame Duck Industries in the mid 1980s, unemployed workers – more than 800,000 of them – were encouraged to resort to social security.

A 'coach and horses' was driven through the social security system as ex-industrial workers were warehoused in long-term unemployment and state benefits. Up until then, the social security system was used largely for the invalided, the old and the temporarily ill. But after the government, in order to weaken trade unions and reduce wages, wrecked Britain's major industries, social security became a safety net to stave off rebellion. Unfortunately, it was a safety net of concrete. Few people bounced back out of its embrace.

This grew a class of 'workless' people, who often passed their inactivity onto their children, creating cross generational levels of dependency and despondency.

Among others the NHS is catering for a large group of people – the permanently workless – who did not exist previously. And because the NHS no longer functions as it was intended to, which was to prevent illness, it deals with an increasing number of people with bad health, high levels of inactivity and related health problems. Hence the behemoth increase of the NHS. Drawing as it does from its misguided mission, which is largely just to provide when it is needed, there cannot but be an increasing demand for their services. Until the NHS becomes a true 'health' service, rather than continuing as a 'sick' service, we will have the vast draws upon the time and talents of its employees. Until prevention becomes central to how the service works, the NHS will remain underfunded and unable to fulfil its mandate to make Britain healthier.

Until the NHS faces up to the high level of personal bodily abuse that exists in the 'workless' sector of the community and its children, we will have more of the same. Unless the NHS turns its attention to prevention, demands on it will increase and put untold pressure on its budget.

Without poverty, a vast part of the expenditure of the NHS would not be needed. Without this new group of 'workless' people created over the last thirty years, the NHS could be doing other things: more prevention and less emergency.

Poverty gives doctors and nurses a job to do. Their time would be better spent on protecting people from preventable diseases, or on research, or on giving a better service to people who are ill through accident, birth defects and age.

The NHS's vast 'customer' base relies on the workless and their families. The growth of morbid obesity is largely a class based development with obesity tied to long term unemployment.

The health industry, like the crime and justice industries, relies on the continuing presence of poverty in our communities. Poverty keeps the wheels turning, no different from the era when 'Satanic Mills' were run by the destitute driven into abject servitude. But are there others who rely on poverty in society, who rely on the 'necessity of poverty' to turn a coin? Who requires poverty to exist in order to make use of what it throws up?

I too have contributed to the increasing gap between rich and poor, I too have thrived because of poverty along with hundreds of thousands of others.

A few years ago I was interviewed by the author of a book about the woman who helped me throughout my early years. Barbara Wooton was one of four women who broke the monopoly that kept the House of Lords exclusively male until 1958. Prime Minister Harold Macmillan appointed Barbara Wooton because of her reputation for helping the poor. She was a juvenile magistrate before whom I appeared six times between the ages of ten and sixteen. Two years after her ennobling, she sentenced me to a 'short, sharp shock'. She put me on probation aged ten. She sent me to the Crown Court aged fifteen because of a more serious charge. And she returned me to my reformatory after I had run away, stolen a car and smashed it up.

Without poverty, Barbara Wooton would not have been put in the Upper House. Her whole life's work was around poverty. And she was one of those people who find their calling in helping people who were poor. She was a magistrate because she felt she could help people like me to turn away from crime and wrongdoing.

I hated the woman. I hated all she stood for: a woman who made her life out of the poor, and she becomes one of the most important social innovators in the country. Therefore, I did not mince my words with the author. As far as I was concerned, she was a parasite. The interviewee thanked me for my comments and left.

I had a very strange feeling afterwards. If Baronness Wooton needed the poor, did I not also need the poor? I may have come from poverty, a part of the problem becoming a part of the solution, but wasn't my new prosperity and purpose linked in with poverty?

At the age of forty-five, I started The Big Issue and began working with groups all over the world. We developed a street paper movement and brought work to the homeless. We were a 'hand up, not a hand out.' We were opposed to the idea that the poor should be made comfortable through street aid. We believed work increased peoples chance of getting out of need and helped establish independent lives.

I was a provider for the homeless and through their plight I could put to good use my skills and abilities that otherwise would have remained dormant. I had found my metier, my purpose. And I did so in a similar way to how Baronness Wooton had many decades before.

There is a vast array of bodies and groups who work for the benefit of the poor. Without poverty they may never been created, giving work to many people, including myself. The Big Issue has helped countless professionals in TV, journalism and radio to cut their teeth and then move on. Worldwide, thousands of homeless people have been aided into work and off streets. At the same time, professionals have used us to find lucrative and meaningful jobs.

Poverty is rich in drama, allowing film makers and TV creators the chance to portray 'real life'. In fact, poverty is seen as 'real life' to us living outside it, needing vicarious trips into the imagery of poverty to understand it. We become tourists in the kind of poverty imagined by film and programme makers. One could barely imagine a 'realist' film about a church organist in a Cotswold village, all cream teas and middle class manners. No, 'realism' must be gritty and concern those who struggle and are in various stages of holding on or failing. A film maker like Ken Loach had devoted the whole of his professional life to making films about people excluded from prosperity and middle class life.

Loach stands in the tradition of 'The New Cinema', mainly making films set in the North of England. *A Taste of Honey* (1961) and *Saturday Night Sunday Morning* (1960) were Southern films of Northern stories. Largely public school and university educated directors went north to get closer to 'reality', producing some of the most interesting films of the period that tapped into the ignominies thrown up by poverty. *This Sporting Life* was probably the best of these renderings of the exoticism of the Northern working class, a world away from Southern plenty.

Ken Loach's *Kes* (1969) is a superb rendering of this largely tough and honest North. Loach is a grammar school and university educated film maker working on a 'real' subject. The book by northern writer Barry Hines, *A Kestral for a Knave*, provided the film maker with his launch pad. He had already made his reputation in films about London poverty (including the seminal *Cathy Come Home*), but they showed a defeated poor. Loach has been the most consistent of film makers growing out of this 'realist' school who but for the 'necessity of poverty' would be subject-free. The fact that Loach has turned out some of the best films of the last forty years shows that poverty as subject matter can be utilised creatively. And that the fight to end poverty can be continued using the medium of film.

Culture, like the economy and our own prosperity, rests squarely on the broad backs of the poor. Without them, we are lost. And we are without some of the most interesting cultural manifestations of the modern era.

# 5
# GIVING AND TAKING

'Giving' is the big news in the religious world. To give to people less well off than yourself is key to salvation. Not to give means to be unable to participate in the central credo of the church unless, of course, you are so poor yourself that you are the recipient of others' generosity.

When I was seven, my family broke up. We children ended up in a Catholic orphanage, where we were fed and educated, kept militarily clean and clothed well. We had big clean dormitories, but the experience was so traumatic that it put me off charity for much of my life.

Once out of the orphanage, we moved to a council flat and attended our local school. There, I ran into another side of charity. And that was not as a taker but as a giver. Our teacher gave us each a small box into which we were to put money for children in Africa. I was ten and living in a family that had almost no money. Yet I was expected to get my family to put money into the little collection box. The teacher was vicious about those of us who said we had no money. He kept on and each day reported on the progress of the children and their fundraising. Eventually, on the last possible day of collecting, having failed to convince my parents and neighbours to put money in, I stole two shillings from my mother's purse.

This did not save me from humiliation. The teacher emptied my box in front of the class and suggested that two shillings was such a paltry amount I need not have bothered. My mother discovered the missing money and beat me for my dishonesty. Like a lot of poor people, she had no sentimental feeling for what I had done with the money. She would have been happier if I had used it on myself.

Imagine churches without the poor. Imagine what would happen if any of the political solutions that have been bandied about in the last hundred years had cleared the slums, emptied the sweat factories and cleaned up the doorways of poverty forever. Imagine what religion would do in the wake of such a transformation.

How could good Christians, for instance, express themselves in the face of their beliefs with no one to give help to, to give alms to? The needy, the invalid, the poor, have always been the backbone of the churches' purpose. Take out of that equation the need to help people and the church loses its central mission.

What religion has done throughout history is provide us with our morality. Morality that is firmly based on our relationship with poverty. If Make Poverty History had worked its magic, the church would have no buttressing.

As we know, poverty is not going anywhere fast. The church need not worry about that. What the church does need to worry about it is the way in which it encourages charity.

Much of the aid that the church offers comes from acts of generosity. As the Bible says, 'It is better to give than to receive.' The Church continuously reinforces that there are two kinds of people in life: those in need and those who need to give. One might even see these two kinds of people as different species. One gives to the needy. The other receives from the prosperous.

The Church makes no value judgements on the people in need. It is above judgement, might run the argument. Even the fallen and the needy are God's children.

This 'hands off' attitude creates one of the biggest problems we face today. Giving unconditionally, as a hand out, can lead to dependency. Giving without purpose, other than to bring relief, can spoil the chance for people to get out of need. The needy remain a different species. They remain in need. And they remain forever appealing for alms from those not in need.

I would suggest that much giving does the giver more good than the receiver. The receiver may receive temporary respite. But does it do anything for any length of time in the course of their life? Why does it say in the Bible that it is better to give than to receive?

Think about it: the giver always has better social and health circumstances. Holidays, worldly goods. And the recipients have their need.

Christianity creates the idea that goodness and giving are one and the same thing, irrespective of how that affects the recipient. The church appeals to us to give, yet never accepts the responsibility that giving prolongs dependency. When I started The Big Issue street paper that got homeless people working and not begging, I ran into the limitations of the cultural, philosophical and intellectual power of Christian giving. On every front as I tried to turn needy people into independent agents in their own lives – through work – I found people trying to turn us back simply into a giving machine.

As a former beggar, I can state that begging was not good for me. It always gave me a reason to return to the streets, to look pathetic and lost. To rely on the generosity of strangers. And to postpone the time when I would have to take charge and change my life.

In 1998, the new Prime Minister Tony Blair proudly boasted 'that we live in an age of giving.' He said this in his usual upbeat manner that radiated an apparent aura of goodness. There was always something devotional about Blair, suggesting that he had captured the mood of the country.

I was in an argumentative frame of mind because he contradicted all the work that I had been doing for the previous seven years. I had been working on getting poor people working, and it was difficult to keep the momentum up. So I asked the *Guardian* for space to reply to Blair's giving claim. My message was simple: if we live in an age of giving would that not suggest that we also live in an age of taking? Had he tried being a taker? Did he know what kind of life a taker ends up with?

Well intentioned but damaging 'giving' can delay the flight from poverty. Helping poor requires providing them with opportunity, not giving them handouts.

The biggest piece of giving though was not from the Church. As I shall describe later it was from the State. The State had turned into the biggest giver of 'hand outs' but not 'hand ups', through the benefit system. Institutional giving on such a vast scale that it dwarfed much of the work of people like me trying to create chances of moving people away from dependency. Blair's legacy, hotly disputed by his followers, has an increasing trail of this cack-handed giving called 'benefit'.

Christianity in its various forms operates a duality over the poverty: it expects the 'giving class' of people to be upright and independent and moral, but it never expects the same from the poor. The poor, God's true children, the righteous inheritors in the next world, the truly true of the world, can be commiserated with and can be sentimentalised over. Depriving them of independent livelihood institutionalises them as a segregated and dependent sub-group.

As someone who has passed from one group to the other, from poverty into comfort with a disposable income, I object to this facile view of the poor. Seeing the poor, as I have said, as almost another species perpetuates their poverty.

So when Blair, a self-declared Christian prime minister, exults us to give, he is doing little more than what Christianity has done for so long. Never undermining the class divisions in society. Never fighting for the poor to get out of poverty. Forever weighing them down with the need of the 'giver' to give. And by that, they guarantee their own mission and their own redemption.

I am sure this sounds like crude shorthand to some people, because numerous Christians do not believe in giving handouts. Some insist on hand-ups. The great universities often have Christian intentions in giving bursaries and scholarships to bright children with no money. A famous TV historian I met once was most adamant about how he was lifted out of a working class council estate by an endowment from a college that had been founded on Christian principles.

I know many Christians who believe that the best way of helping the poor is to show them a way out of poverty. And that means training and support. But the vast body of the Christian Churches preach a debilitating 'poverty syrup' which can only slow the process of people winning control of their lives. There is only one cure to poverty: to get out.

We should give constructively and consciously. We should give not merely to bring day-to-day relief. At times we have to give this kind of aid, but we need to move our giving on to changing and reconstructing lives, so that they can then escape poverty and obtain the kind of social mobility we encourage in our own children.

Although most people do not attend church and do not see their giving as a particularly Christian act, our morality and our concerns for the needy are marinated in a past that stems from the church. Because of that, we cannot escape the 'poverty syrup' that churches often practise. It is up to us to reform our charitable giving so that it is not a way for proving our moral goodness so much as to end the injustice perpetuated by begging.

# 6
# THE POVERTY OF POLITICS

In this chapter I want to discuss why politicians would be lost without poverty. Few politicians build their reputations without suggesting that they are there for the poor as much as the rich, as much for the uncomfortable as the comfortable.

I do not want to discuss the nature of their politics, but how if you extract and throw away poverty you are left with a political husk, a shell without contents.

Poverty is the driving force behind politics and has dominated the debate for over two hundred years.

I wrote an article about ten years ago where I used the term 'Povitics' for the melding of politics and poverty. Nothing has changed in ten years to make me feel that poverty is not still the big reason, real or imagined, why people get involved in politics.

We are still debating poverty because the politicians have not yet Made Poverty History. That is why we must examine how useful politicians are when it comes to poverty, but before that I have a story to tell you.

The children of haute bourgeois conservatives seemed thick on the ground in Paris when I fled there from British police in 1967. But unlike their parents with their splendid flats and big pianos, and pied à terre on the Côte d'Azur, they were Marxists. They went back at night to the plenty, but their hearts were in the meetings at the Mutualies, big left wing debating halls, and discussing Sartre and Che Guevara.

Celestine was seventeen, and I was twenty-one. I looked like an imitation Che, though I had not been fighting oppressive regimes in the jungle highlands. I had been hiding from the police, getting drunk and taking drugs. I was a thief, a conman and a sexual opportunist. Celestine was a haute bourgeois child of plenty, determined to become a Sartrean Marxist.

We got off to a bad start, when I blamed Jews and blacks for most of the worlds problems. She excoriated me so completely that I realised that I had to change my verbal repertoire to get anywhere with her. So I sought her advice. In a kind of moralising blitzkrieg, she castigated me for being a 'piece of shit on the foot of imperialism', a dupe and a cover for American oppression.

She did a fine job. I was soon saying all the right things. For mouthing the rhetoric of world revolution, I was allowed to undress her. She went on about Comrade Sartre and Comrade Beauvoir in my small room near the Gare du Nord. And she lectured me on the poor and oppressive role of capital.

Although I found the lines often stuck in my throat, I said what she wanted to hear. Gradually, as if by osmosis, or by total submergence in a Paris so full of radical young people, I began to adopt the ideas as mine. I found myself arguing with Celestine that we should do more than talk about ending poverty. We should go and rob some banks and kill some of the bourgeoisie. She was horrified at my idea to spill blood for the cause and drew back from the abyss.

As far as she was concerned, Sartre had it right about poverty. We had to support struggles throughout the world. But what we should do was argue and fight in the colleges and universities, the schools and the cafés, for this new revolutionary society. We would make trips to places in Montparnasse and near the Sorbonne to see Sartre and Simone de Beauvoir. I cannot remember ever setting eyes on the great man, but I began to feel that Sartre to Celestine was what Jesus had been to me when I was a boy: a catchall, someone that ironed out all the contradictions in life. A talisman, the old man was though, little more than a talker.

I left Paris a few months later, convinced that world revolution was the way forward. I explained my ideas to a soldier on the boat train. He was outraged, especially by my support for the Vietcong. I pulled a knife on him, and he ran over to get the train stopped. It didn't stop. I feared that when I got to Dover I would be arrested for my past wrongdoings as well as some new ones.

I wanted confrontation. At last, I had found the key to my own disturbed life lay in blaming the bastards who had made me and my family poor for centuries. From the Irish Catholic and Protestant poor, I was a cipher of social failure and now I would exact some revenge. The only thing I managed to do was rob shops and cause fires. But at some stage I would get drawn into proper revolution, and then I could make a real mark.

Fortunately, a Trotskyist group in London addressed my romantic strain of direct action, of blood and guts murder that I felt needed to be exacted on the bourgeoisie. Its members challenged me. How serious was I? Was I just working out my angst and personal 'fuckups' by turning it into masturbatory political action. Once again, I was excoriated, and this time it stuck. And for the next two decades I was either in the movement or around it. Most of the seventies and much of the eighties I was a foot soldier for the revolutionary group and learned application and dedication to one cause and the art of working all hours for it.

One of my areas of responsibility was to recruit young boys and girls to our youth movement. I worked in the Shepherd's Bush and Notting Hill area, back to the area where I was born. Among others, I recruited a young girl who went to Holland Park Comprehensive School by Notting Hill.

Holland Park Comprehensive School was filled with a careful balance of film makers, musicians and politicians, mixed with the children of the working classes. Tony Benn, who had gone to Westminster School, one of Britain's best public schools, famously sent his children to Holland Park Comprehensive. The Benn family's class allegiance had changed when Tony's father jumped ship from the Liberals to Labour. The son sided with his father, became a Labour Party man, and rejected his privileged beginnings. He bought a big run down house in Notting Hill, became an MP for Bristol South East and had a reputation as a left winger.

Subsequently, it was not surprising that he put his children through the new social experiment of abolishing the class system by putting them in a state school. The Benn children have spoken about how good the comprehensive school was. It released them from the narrow upper classes that they came from. But how much of their conversion was any more than appearance?

Tony's son Hilary Benn is an English patrician. Although he went to a comprehensive state school, he retained the manners and culture of a highly privileged member of the more fortunate classes. The failure to turn him into a man of the people, something his father has spent most of his life trying to achieve, symbolised the tokenism of much post-war politics.

Like Sartre, Benn needed the poor to endorse his position. To give him credence, and I would say direction. His politics is a further sign that without poverty many politicians would be rudderless, lost in a sea of actions that lead nowhere in particular.

Many politicians, both in and out of the parliamentary system, define themselves by what they will do if they ever achieve real power. Tony was a typical politician who used his commitment to coming to the rescue of the poor as the leitmotif of his political life. Yet there is more poverty in England after all Blair's years in Downing Street than there was when he arrived in 1997.

Politicians over the last two hundred years or more, certainly since the French Revolution, have claimed they would eradicate poverty. Marxism is the most obvious political philosophy to counteract poverty and Lenin was one of the most famous exponents of using poverty as a political battering ram. Like the French Revolution, without the inchoate masses of the sans-cullottes, none of the big changes in recent centuries would have taken place. Only by having the masses stirred and fired up to rip up the old system was it possible to institute radical change.

Without hungry workers and peasants, soldiers and sailors, there would have been no Bolshevik Revolution.

Poverty is the maker and unbreaker. Lenin was unable to feed all the workers and peasants. The reactionary growth of Stalinism and its atrocious record of oppression and counter-revolution was the outcome of not being able to address poverty. It did not help that not one person on the Bolsheviks' Central or Political bureaus knew how markets worked. Most had only a highly ideological understanding. This ignorance cost them the revolution and the chance to remake the world anew.

Poverty was the great king maker of the last two hundred years. But it was also the undoer. As Lenin could not staunch his revolution from bleeding to death, and party parliamentarians did not bring the new world of social equality, poverty is as alive as it ever was. And why it still stalks the debating chambers of the world. And controls the gun, the bomb and the ballot box. Religious wars may flare but the backdrop is poverty: homelessness, hunger, deprivation, disease and ignorance.

Poverty was the flame behind the First World War. It was the backdrop of Hitler's ascendancy, and it was the reason that his thousand year Reich lasted only twenty-two. Fear of poverty drove the creation of the big European empires that fought the First World War. It drives us still and will be the big fight in the future.

Because the best minds have proposed fantasies to help the poor rather than to eliminate poverty, we will pay the price of this gross misuse of our physical, cultural and intellectual treasure. Now is not the time for any more false gods, nor false illusions. But that is another chapter.

# 7
# FALSE HELPERS

I heard the other day that even though there were over seven billion people on the planet, they would all fit, shoulder to shoulder, on Tasmania. Tasmania's land mass is 62,409 square kilometres.

When I was a young man, my fellow Marxists and I loved saying the world's population could fit, shoulder to shoulder, on the Isle of Wight. The Isle of Wight is 384 square kilometres.

We had our reasons for using the Isle of Wight at a time when the world's population was about 3½ billion. It is the same reason, I believe, why some now use Tasmania: to show that there are not too many people in the world.

One thing the radical supporters of the poor wish to avoid is saying 'the poor are having too many children'. Radicals will fight you to the death over this. For if you are telling the poor to have less children, by suggesting there are too many people on the planet, then Tasmania and the earlier Isle of Wight works wonders in proving that they are not.

So, leave the poor alone.

What the middle classes, who make up most of the radicals and Marxists, really do not want to be doing is telling the poor how many children they should have. Why, runs the argument, should the wealthy and comfortable be able to have all the children in the world, therefore controlling their fertility, while the poor can't?

One thing Marxists and assorted radicals don't want to be seen doing is talking down to or moralizing about the poor. The poor have too many constraints already aimed at them.

The problem with this argument is that it flies in the face of something very simple: and that is that the more children you likely you are to stay impoverished.

Many environmentalists will also tell you that the damage done by the increase in mouths on the planet by poor people is a lot less than the damage done by the comfortable classes. For instance, it takes thirty-nine times more energy to keep one comfortable American in energy and resources than it does a rural Bangladeshi. Countless numbers like this prove in some ways that we need more Bangladeshi's – i.e., poor peasants – than we need high energy spending and consuming Americans.

There may be some truth in that. This argument is rather fatuous if it is used to protect and defend, rather than tackle, the issue of people giving birth to more children than they can reasonably afford to look after.

My mother had six children who survived, and a few miscarriages. Her body showed the marks of her poverty, and she did not live long enough to enjoy the fruits of her womb. Physically wrecked by births, added to by the need to feed so many mouths on the wages of a building worker, she never had a life of her own. At one time, she was an all night cleaner who sent three of her children to school in the morning before collapsing into bed and collecting them later.

She never voted. She never had any time for herself. She never went on holiday, except for the last few years of her life when she had a week each year in a caravan. She smoked, her greatest joy, and that helped her die at the age of 52. She was a skeleton of a woman, worn out, not just by the cancer, but by the daily labour of keeping body and soul together.

Radicals are frightened of telling the poor not to have more children, because it looks as if they are judging them. But I do not take such a detached view. I have seen the damage done to a woman's spirit by having too many children and no life for herself. Surrounding us in our slums were similar women who had no life because they had too many children.

So those who do not wish to 'lecture' the poor on their fertility unwittingly keep them poor and worn out. This, of course, may not apply to peasant farmers in the third world, who have many children in the home that some will survive to support them in their old age. But the whole question of fertility needs to be seen as decreasing a persons chance of getting out of poverty.

In the twentieth century, the British middle classes increased by about seventy percent. If you meet middle class people who do not wish to 'talk down' to the poor, they are often only a few generations away from poverty themselves. How did they make the transformation into middle class life? Previous generations 'burnt the candle at both ends', they studied, worked, and got themselves out of poverty. And one of the things they did was avoid having big families themselves.

How many times have I heard something like the following: 'Yes, my (grand)dad came form a family of eight, but he studied and worked hard and got into the professions.' When you ask how many children dad or granddad had, you will find it was nearly always the middle class standard two.

By putting the argument that the poor should have all the children they want, you are in fact condemning them to something that you may well have escaped yourself a few generations ago.

Radicalism and Marxism are loose terms now. Their competing tendencies contradict one other. In Kerala, India, about forty years ago, a Marxist government decided to do something about the appalling level of illiteracy in the state. So they instituted a literacy programme. Within a few decades Kerala had the highest literacy in India – among all people, not just the middle classes.

If you go to India now, you will find a vast number of nurses and doctors come from Kerala. Accountants and professional people from there are also increasing. Social mobility is the reality.

What has happened to the birth rate among these formerly illiterate people? Whereas once the average family unit was just over nine children per family it is now down to about two. Literacy enabled more of the people to become educated and join the middle classes. Presumably, their children will become radicals and Marxists, if they so chose. And begin to fight against poverty.

We can understand why right-wingers, of a certain kind, call for the lessening of poor populations with big families. They do not want the burden on their taxes. There are also many right-of-centre environmentalists who – rather than turn their spotlight on the wealthy westerners with their thirty-nine times greater energy and resource consumption than a Bangladeshi – want fewer poor people.

Even the right-wingers, like Marxists, are not uniform in their condemnation. In America, even for the poorest family, the pro-lifers want to end the rights of women to terminate pregnancy. So even in this area there is little consistency among the political wings.

It is understandable why people want to protect the poor from exploitation and moralising, but surely condemning people to a lifetime of no life, like my mother, is not productive.

Incidentally there is only one place where the poor can and do have as many children as they want and do not starve in the streets for it. That is in the metropolitan centres of North America to some extent, and in Europe. Because of a false belief in the powers of benefits, many people who would have left poverty and joined the seventy percent now in the middle classes, are left to rot. Welfare has become on too many occasions its opposite.

# THE NECESSITY OF POVERTY

Ed Milliband, a decent defender of the poor, made the point to me that 'social mobility' was not the be-all and end-all in curing poverty. We had been on the same TV programme, and he spoke before me. He believed that we needed to give more support to the poor, whereas I said that the only cure for poverty was to get out of it.

You cannot and should not maintain people in poverty. It is erroneous and bad for poor people.

If Mr Milliband's father and mother had arrived in the UK as refugees from Nazism in the 1940s and been welcomed with social security and social housing, would he be running the Labour Party? Or would he not be condemned to a life of need on some sink estate, with no education worth talking about? The predictability of failure that goes with receiving benefit is an outrage against human rights. Yet so many people want to warehouse the poor in benefit for the most well intentioned reasons.

We have to free the poor of the whip hand of the one percenters. We have to free ourselves of a dependency on the products of the one percenters. We have to free the poor from their exploiters and well wishers who keep them from gaining an exit out of poverty.

# 8
# THE SYSTEM!

The system we all live under is finely balanced. It has us all in its grip:

> The rich man in his gated community.
> The protester at the gates.
> The company selling the product.
> The poor man making it.
> And the consumer consuming it.

It is such a neat mother-fucker of a system that it's water tight. Everyone has a role in this system. Nothing is wasted. Every church, shop, town hall, mugger, lawyer, and human rights advocate plays its role this system that shows no signs of defaulting.

All keep the much prized balance. The poor, when they occasionally tire or revolt or riot, are led into dead ends of political radicalism that keep the system going. The children of the comfortable, and at times the uncomfortable, are led into similar cul-de-sacs of protest and anger, laced with the right amount of activism.

Newspapers, TV and now the Internet supply us with the information about the iniquities of poverty, greed, murder, despoliation and corruption. Remember that these pieces of poisonous information are themselves pieces of product. How many people do you know who are obsessed with knowing the news but do little with this encyclopaedia of mayhem and murder? Because it is not knowledge per se, it is news. Even serious stuff is gossip. Riots in Tottenham become sources of gossip that are passed around as if they happened in another country that was being burnt and scarred by social collapse.

There are many hundreds of thousands of charities, NGOs and political activist groups who let the steam dissipate or do some amount of fixing, just enough to make us feel that in our time on earth we have done something. We have our tireless saints who devote countless years to help those who need help, yet because the system works so mother-fuckingly well, there are always more people in need than it is possible to help.

There are always death row activists and support groups who try heroically to help, and they do help, but there is always someone else who has been atomized by modern life who needs the next bit of help.

The system is so good at pretending that it listens that it can keep the rich man in his castle and the poor man at his gate.

Even revolutionaries are involved in the system. Even the reddest of revolutionary doctrines never coalesces to break the system. Like churches and religious cults, they put the Promised Land on hold.

If we want to do something, we have to find a way of understanding this system and why it defeats us all. We have to find a way not to perpetuate this system. And to do that, we have to tear up almost every rule book ever written. In the end we will have to defeat the system.

Even for those who want things to carry on, this is an ecosystem that is breaking down. There is no long term chance of human life and the natural world carrying on the way it is.

The poorest man I ever knew was my father. If there ever was a system man, it was him. He actually understood that he was a part of some giant system that required him to work endless hours on building sites. He even understood that if he did not go into the Princess Alexander public house in Notting Hill where we lived, and deposit half his wages in the till, something might fall apart. Unlike my mother, he would never rail against Jews, because some of them gave him work. And he made sure we went to church, although he said it was 'a load of old bollocks'. Why? Because, when he married a Catholic he had signed a piece of paper to say we would be brought up Catholic. And that was the system.

He kept telling me, as he saw me get wilder and madder and angrier and more outraged at the system, that it was to no avail. The system always won. Whether it was 'that bearded cunt', referring to Fidel Castro, or some Labour leader becoming the new Prime Minister.

He said one night in a light mood, when I asked him why he smoked, 'If I don't, then think of all those people who'll be out of pocket.' Later, when I was hiding from the police in Bristol, I noticed the imposing faux gothic Wills Memorial building and library for graduates and undergraduates. I mused for a moment on how many cigarettes it takes to build a library for middle class students. My father made me realise there was a system, and it worked however many times I threw bricks at it.

That was the system. And it all fitted together. Even the way my father kept the Earl of Iveagh in race horses was a part of that.

To my father the system was natural. If you did not work, you did not get paid. If you agreed to do something, you did it. Whoever the bosses were, they handed out the work. That was the end of it.

But I could not accept this fatalism. I got involved in protest politics and eventually Marxist politics and stayed involved for almost two decades. And out of this came my understanding that there was a system. And that it involved everybody; left, right and centre.

Of course the system breaks down. And Arab Spring or a sinking of Tesco happens. But until we understand that system consciously then we will be guilty of repeating its mistakes. Until we combine our anger, our energies, our efforts, the systemic undermining of our efforts will continue. And the environment and the world of life and people will wilt.

The system leads us into dead ends. It leads us into repetition and acceptance. Without a full analysis of this system, with its inbuilt ways for us to let us let off steam, then our passage through life will be limited.

# 9
# SUMMATION

I hope in this short work I have successfully underlined how we are all implicated in the continuity of poverty. That our society, our marketplaces, are angled to make the most out of the poor. So that when you read or hear the inane comments of the supposedly well educated saying that 'there is no working class' anymore, you might quibble. The wholesale diminishing of the lives of the largest part of the world's population to that of servers of our appetites, and supplying us with work and purpose, needs to be faced. To do so we need to get rid of some illusions along the way.

Be critical of the one percenters if you wish; tax them and limit their so called 'greed'. It will not change much for the poor. Blame bankers and hit their bonuses, which again only marginally affects the poor.

Until we act on the vast consumer power that is within our own hands we are fooling ourselves. If we seriously want to close the gap between the rich and the poor, we better stop making the rich richer. We better stop trading with the people whose lifestyles we find vile, selfish, or whatever pejorative forms we wish to lay on them.

We have to realise the collective power we hold in our hands. Only collective actions have made changes in the world, whether defeating Nazism or eradicating smallpox. We may choose to make political noises and gestures, but they will not make the difference we require.

Protest has been the mainstay of much political action since the Second World War. It has not necessarily been the most effective. Think of 1968, when many young French students joined with some workers to take on the French state. The 'insurrection' led nowhere. Selflessness was sacrificed at the altar of commerce and normality. The young grew up to become part of the system they despised. They were incorporated. Protest does this. It makes noises that never match the reality that grows out of it. Good intentions show another generation of the young making the impotent mistakes of their forefathers.

We need a deeper, less off-the-shelf protest politics if we are to get anywhere in getting rid of poverty. We will have to place ourselves right in the centre of the equation.

I work with homeless people who have had everything thrown at them. What often holds them back is actually not what was done to them, but what they end up doing to themselves and their inability to hold themselves accountable. Hence, they often blame everyone else for their poverty rather than accept the fact that they will remain homeless until they put themselves at the centre of their problem.

I would suggest that we have to take the same attitude. Until we recognize the power for change rests with us, we will change nothing. It is the collective power of our abilities and inabilities to change that we must recognise.

## SUMMATION

Until we invent new means of buying and selling that do not enrich one group at the expense of another, we are going nowhere. Until we go back to the marketplace and reform it, the poor will not get a living wage and we will continue to increase the gap between rich and poor.

The reform of the marketplace around fair trade is the only way forward. That means buying products so that people can feed and educate and care for their children. All the Robin Hood taxes in the world will change nothing.

The first thing we need to do is understand what is going on. Grasp the differences between capitalism now in the first decades of the twenty-first century, and the capitalism of the last two centuries. Why? Because much of the political activism reflects the 'old' thinking as if we were still in the nineteenth or early twentieth centuries. We have political traditions that were created in 1789, when sans culottes overwhelmed the *ancien régime* for the political advantage of the radical bourgeoisie. We still use the politics of protest and single issue politics that have grown out of that tradition.

In order to offer a good prognosis we need a full diagnosis. We have to see beyond the appearance of things, to the truth.

We have to know what or who the enemy is. We have to understand how trade works and not simply blame the one percenters.

Samuel Taylor Coleridge pointed out during a lecture he gave on slavery at the end of the 18th century: if you don't like slavery then don't buy the product of slavery – sugar.

## THE NECESSITY OF POVERTY

Something similar applies here. If you don't like the gap between rich and poor, don't buy from the one percenters.

I have stressed my culpability in this system for one reason and one reason alone. I don't want to do what most people do. That is, define myself by the failures of others. To see the problems as only caused by others. This is, the classic Judeo-Christian way of moralising. Take any middle class person and what you tend to get is a moraliser with someone else pissing on the chips. Someone else being responsible. Whether it is blaming the bankers, or the McDonaldization of the world, people want let themselves off the hook and put someone else on it.

We are the recipients of the growth of the gap, as well as the one percenters. If you add up what we get out of the poor and what the one percenters get, I assure you that we collectively get the lion's share.

But this is not the usual limp-wristed reworking of 'he who is free of sin cast the first stone'. That's another good use of the bible to make sure that people do nothing. Rather it is to drive home the reality: we collectively have the power. We have the power to stop patronising the one percenters and move our business to other places. If we want to stop the gap growing between rich and poor, we have to pull out of the arrangement between us and the one percenters.

Mark my words: it may be sexy to have a Robin Hood tax. It may sound tough to take money from the one percenters, but it will not improve the lot of the poor more than marginally. The four hundred billion pounds shown in the *Sunday Times* UK rich list is nothing compared to the financial power that exists within us, collectively. We can determine the success or failure of a business, however many tax breaks they get. It is our power, our strength as consumers, to make the whole thing work for the one percenters. And, likewise, we have the power to undo them. But that will take some serious organising.

Think on another thing: the combined power of the pension funds, in terms of wealth, dwarfs one percenters, banks and governments. Thirty trillion pounds is floating out there trying to make a fast buck for our pensions, whether those pensions are for a trade union, a university or an individual. A trade union in Norway lost a sizable part of its income and capital from investing in the toxic debts of sub-prime housing in America.

The need for people to have security and a good income in their retirement makes fools of us all if we seek purity. Capitalism has moved on since the days when Marx could claim to understand its machinery. Consumerism is the new universal capitalism, and none of us, not even the poor, is aloof from this post-war reality. We live in a world where the 'necessity of poverty' hovers over our every move. It is a destructive reality that seeks urgent understanding and attention.

Tolstoy tells a great story that illustrates our need to know about things before we judge them. One hot day, Tolstoy was walking through the countryside and he saw a mad man in the distance throwing his arms around. Tolstoy was vexed. Why did no one look after the mentally ill? He got closer and cursed again the fact that people did not look after the weak. As he got even closer, he decided to do something for this poor mad man on this hot day in the middle of a scorching summer.

He got so close to the man that he could see that he was … sharpening a scythe.

The man was not mad. He seemed mad when Tolstoy was far from him and was speculating on the man's madness. Seeing him up close, Tolstoy realised that what the man was doing was perfectly rational.

When you have all the information necessary, you can see the truth.

One of the big problems today is that we are swamped by information. We are inundated with data and opinions, with breaking news, reports and investigations. Yet we still do not know much about many things that we are asked to pass judgement on.

The great financial meltdown of a few years ago came upon us and destroyed much wealth and much security. Yet how much do we know about it? How much are we aware of so to be able to pass judgement and decide what to do about things in the future?

By now you may have realised that I don't believe in using greed as an excuse. I might be fooling myself. Maybe life is all greed. Maybe when they said that 'nature was red in tooth and claw', they should have also said, 'and it's greedy also.' Likewise, I have never been very good with evil. Evil to me is a catchall. Once you've applied it, you can then stop thinking about it.

## SUMMATION

Or so it seems to me. To me, greed and evil are used to excuse, explain, file, dump. And stop thinking.

Now here's the problem, partner: if you want to talk about the gap between rich and poor, the uneven distribution of wealth, property, clean air, clean water, underwear, you name it, without slinging in words like 'greed' and 'evil', you are making hard work for yourself.

I'd say it's a bit like getting in a rowboat without the oars. You have to work overtime and then some to get anywhere anytime soon.

Here's the contradiction: in spite of having those two words thrown around from pulpit to battlefield, from bedroom to boardroom, we still seem to have a lot of it. So while we have been fighting the good fight against the evilness of greed, or the greediness of evil, it seems, by all reports, from the *Guardian* to the BBC, from the pages of the prayer books to the *Daily Mail*, to be ubiquitous!

Now, if not using 'greed' and 'evil' is like going rowing without oars, what is it like if you also ditch, jettison, throw overboard, and defenestrate moralizing? Where does that leave your critique, your indictment, your *J'accuse!?*

That would be a Houdini of a job to get out of that, and at the same time prove that poverty is such and such, and needs to be addressed. It's easier to present it as a story of moral collapse or an evil expression of greed.

Now this is all getting to sound like recklessness, especially, lastly, if you add another encomium: taking morality out of the equation, taking evil and greed out of the discussion, you now add another no-no: sentimentality.

That is, a sentimental attachment to the poor. Throw that away with greed, evil and morality!

If you do the above, and still try to prove that poverty can be eliminated, then you may well be a fool.

I am a fool, but I am going show you poverty in a new light. Let's try and see our way through the darkness that surrounds it.

I have young children who ask questions about poverty and the poor. 'Dad, why are there poor people in the street?' I would rather be asked to take an uneducated guess at what the Big Bang theory is or how computers work. No, you are not onto a winner when you try to tell your children why there are poor people on the street. I manage the short hand version, rather than the long list of causes and counter causes, and sub-causes.

I never indulge in complexity. But I hope that when my children grow up they will enter the fray and work it out for themselves – minus evil, greed and moralising. And without an ounce of sentimentality towards the poor!

I hope also they get around to reading what their daddy did to help people understand that it is not all cakes and ale. It is not explicable using the usual tools. The sooner we move from demonising the problem and the rich, the sooner we may get to the place that the better leaders of the past wanted to lead us.

I come at the problem of poverty from a different place to almost anyone I have ever met. The world of poverty, like the medical profession, and the police, are not run by the onetime poor, or the formerly ill, or the erstwhile criminal.

# SUMMATION

Likewise with poverty, you rarely get people who have been poor ending up writing about ending poverty.

That is not to say that there are not formerly poor people in positions of leadership around poverty. But it is unusual for formerly homeless people to be involved in running homeless groups.

The poor never get to run revolutionary parties, or labour parties, both of which have staked their lives and reputations on ending poverty and releasing the poor from their shackles. It is nearly always the middle classes who run the show.

One of Hercules's tasks was 'cleansing the Augean Stables'. It has come to mean a variation on 'back to the drawing board', or beginning again, or tearing up the old practises and bringing in the new.

Our present political rainbow, from left to right, with liberal variations in the middle, does not meet the requirements of our times. We must take matters into our own hands. We must come up with new ways to tackle poverty.

# 10
# AFTERTHOUGHT

The gestation of this paper owes much to the sight of Nelson Mandela on a large poster in the road I lived in, espousing the need to Make Poverty History. That was eight years ago. I was struck by how strange it was to see an exhortation from the world's most well known freedom fighter to do something quite abstract.

Not to buy a product, or to support a political party. Or to simply send money (though that was one of the campaign's goals). No, but to sign up to rewriting the human experience over the next few decades. To rid our lives of the most constant thing that has stalked us since before the days when the Homo sapiens crossed the land bridge out of Africa 125,000 years ago.

Get rid of poverty, consign it to history's dustbin, seemed a worthy cause. It seemed also to be the biggest piece of wishful thinking I had encountered since the year 1968 when I joined the struggle to build a world revolutionary movement and create a classless society.

Added to the sense of strangeness was that I knew the road the vast poster stood in. After forty years I was back living in the one time poverty-stricken streets of my childhood. Back then, Fulham in West London was poor. Forty years later, it was loaded down with wealth, though still mixed in with pockets of need. When I looked at the poster and thought about my own climb out of poverty, I was struck by how real poverty had been to me and how abstract it seemed to be presented by the agency who wanted us all to Make Poverty History.

Was it the same poverty?

This big thing that so entranced and preoccupied so many people. So many politicians, social activists, so many campaigning groups obsessed with it: millions seemed to be involved in this industry of neglect, need and death.

Was this exhortation to rewrite the future for real?

Or was this just another way of getting money out of people and Make Poverty History just the latest brand? Another bright creative's ploy to get us to support a host of charities that conjoined in some representation of a fight against poverty. But really the participating NGOs were simply looking for more money.

Would their gimmick not just fall by the wayside and become old posters, ripped off and replaced by different exhortations to spend on the usual consumer products?

During my own forty year move from poverty to comfort, I have not seen any change to the basic way that poverty is fought. It still was run predominately by people from comfortable backgrounds deciding to do something for those who did not. Outraged by poverty, angered by it, depressed by it, they set to reduce or even obliterate it. They had, it seemed, the best of intentions.

Yet forty years later, poverty still blighted the lives of more people in the world. More than half the world's population had a daily struggle to make ends meet, with a large part hanging on by their fingernails. Poverty seemed as pertinent today as it was yesterday. Still causing our young and talented and concerned to put their lives into eradicating it. Yet it seemed to be an unfillable, bottomless pit, drawing in all of our energies and often much of our wealth.

It occurred to me recently that there seemed to be a very profound observation hidden within all of this activity around poverty. That in the forty years since I was in poverty there had been no sizable move to get those in poverty to be the leaders in the fight against poverty. Of course there were notable exceptions, but they were still exceptions and exceptional people.

Overall, the middle classes still ran poverty. Still ran the responses to it. Still viewed poverty from a position above it. And still came at it as a question of personal choice and not as a question of necessity.

When I went to homeless organisations in 1991 to say that I was going to start a street paper for homeless people, one of the biggest complaints levelled at me was that I was unknown. I did not come at homelessness from having worked my apprenticeship through the ranks of homeless groups. I had no certificates of study or of excellence.

In order to quell some of the distain shown me, I had to checkmate potential critics. I used a simple argument. I said, 'Would it not be good for someone to run a homeless initiative, just as an experiment, who had himself been homeless? Would it not be good to tap into the natural talents and experiences of people who have themselves suffered poverty, abuse, prison, rough sleeping, violence? Not unlike the clients whom you administer to?'

It caused my critics to fall silent. I had pointed out a great anomaly. That for all of the social advantages we had supposedly made in the post-war world, there was little to show in terms of utilising the skills of people who themselves had been a part of the problem.

Everywhere was evidence of committed people who came to poverty second hand, and I was suggesting that we might want to try getting more people who had firsthand experience. That we might want to mix the two kinds of experience.

I decided to write this paper because I believe I might be able to add a different perspective. The perspective of someone who has lived and breathed and struggled out of poverty. Not by nice means, but by using middle class people as stepping stones out of need. I have the unsentimental commitment to the poor that many people who have been poor have. I have the same dislike for dreaminess around poverty that I meet among formerly poor people who have stayed on to help others.

I do not believe in handouts. I believe in hand ups. Therefore I oppose much of the post-war experience that enslaves the poor in dependency, warehousing them in social (in)security.

When I told homeless people they would have to pay for The Big Issue, many of them were outraged. Many argued that homeless people had always been given things for nothing. I said well maybe that's why you are still homeless.

That giving you something for nothing was a sure way to keep you where you are.

I wanted to give the poor what the middle classes had in abundance and used abundantly: the capacity to help themselves. Margaret Thatcher took the 19th century concept of 'self help' and robbed it of its radical content. Gone was the self-help tradition advocated by William Morris, John Ruskin, Robert Owen, leaving only a moralising Samuel Smiles interpretation to foist on people as a High Tory social device.

Self help had been used by Thatcherites as a large stick with which to beat the collective rear of the poor, with Thatcher herself being seen as the heir presumptive of the self help empire. If I were going to be useful to people in need, I was going to have to dust down an even older form of self help and stress its efficacious properties, *sans Tory*. It would need a political fight, especially among radicals who saw the gradual growth of the State as advantageous to those in poverty.

The fight continues. Handouts continue. Unearned income is reserved for only the richest and poorest in society. In between, the middle and working classes have their hands full, earning the lion's share of taxable income. The fight continues as people lose themselves in contradictory practices. Awarding the poor their hard earned money and at the same time goading, encouraging, driving their own children to espouse and use self help ad nauseam.

When the middle classes use money on their own children it is largely a 'hand up'. But the moment they hand it to those in need it largely becomes a 'hand out'. My fight was to encourage the former and dump the latter. To enfranchise the poor in the same way as the middle classes endeavoured to enfranchise their own children. To bring charity back home and treat the poor as if they were your own kith and kin.

We call it 'responsible giving'. Alas, 'responsible giving' remains in the foothills. To reach Himalayan heights may take a revolution.

If we are going to make poverty history, we need to recognise something very basic: many of us depend on poverty for our sustenance, for our social values, for our purpose. Poverty is so entrenched in our lives and our history that we need to recognise how we depend on it for meaning as much as for material things.

*The Necessity of Poverty* has grown out of that belief. The ideas are mine. I cannot say I have shared them with anyone else. If they are laudable, then it is a reflection on how I have managed to go from 'being a part of the problem to becoming a part of the solution'. If they are laughable, then it only proves that yet another person has been defeated by the blandishments of poverty and its corrupting influences.

Of one thing I am convinced: that more people who have lived the experience need the oxygen of promotion. For they can do, dare I suggest, no worse than the present incumbents who run the poverty industry.

I have raised many questions in this paper. I have also endeavoured to supply some answers. I believe the time has come to draw people who started life in the problem, into becoming a part of the solution. Or, as Jesus said: 'Physician, heal thyself.' Which I loosely interpret to mean, 'Those who are ill must make themselves better'. Wow! What a National Health Service we would have if we involved patients in their own wellbeing. And what a great world we would have if we helped the poor to help themselves, and used our aggregated power to that end.